JUNIOR BIOGRAPHIES

Kristen Rajczak
Nelson

SERENA WILLIAMS
TENNIS STAR

Enslow Publishing
101 W. 23rd Street
Suite 240
New York, NY 10011
USA

enslow.com

WORDS TO KNOW

amateur Someone who plays a sport without making money.

compete To seek a prize against others.

debut A first public appearance.

Grand Slam One of the four major professional tennis tournaments. Also, to win all four of these tournaments.

professional Having to do with doing something, such as a sport, for money.

reputation The way someone is seen by others.

rival One of two or more people trying to win what only one person can have.

tournament A sports event at which players compete in a number of contests to find an overall winner.

CONTENTS

Chapter 1
Born to Play

Serena Williams is considered one of the best female athletes of all time. She's won sixty-six singles championships, twenty-two doubles championships, and four Olympic gold medals. According to her father and long-time coach, Richard Williams, these accomplishments are no surprise. He believed early on—and would often tell people—that Serena and her older sister Venus would be stars one day.

Serena Williams is known for her grace on and off the tennis court.

PRACTICE MAKES PERFECT

Serena was born on September 26, 1981, in Saginaw, Michigan, the youngest of five girls. She and Venus had three older half sisters from their mother Oracene's first marriage. When Serena was a baby, her family moved to Compton, a city inside of Los Angeles, California. Compton is an area known for having a lot of crime. The Williams family didn't have a lot of money, but from the age of four, Serena had a tennis racquet in her hand. When Serena was nine, her family moved to West Palm Beach, Florida. There, Richard and Oracene coached their daughters to practice hard. Soon, Serena's serve was over 100 miles (160 kilometers) per hour!

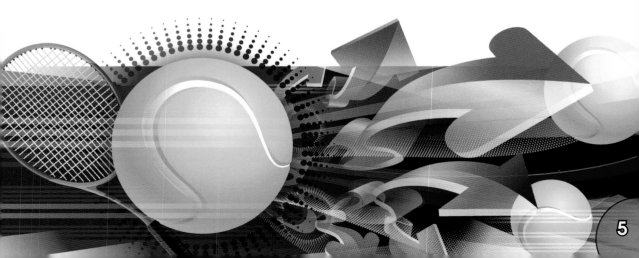

Venus (*left*), and Serena (*right*) worked hard with their father every day.

Unlike many gifted young tennis players, Serena and Venus didn't play much junior-league tennis. But their father talked about his daughters' talent so much, they earned a **reputation** for ruling the court. Then, in 1994, at age fourteen, Venus became a **professional** tennis player. Serena continued practicing as hard as ever and watched her sister make a splash in the tennis world.

FUN FACT

In the early days of tennis, women were required to wear full-length dresses. Serena is well-known for her daring fashion choices on and off the court. A long skirt would certainly make it hard for her to serve!

Venus (in blue) is the older of the two tennis stars. The sisters are nearly unstoppable when they play doubles tennis.

CHAPTER 2
GOING PRO

Serena also wanted to go pro when she turned fourteen. The Women's Tennis Association (WTA) tried to raise the age requirement for pros. Serena fought this decision and made her pro **debut** in 1995 in a **tournament** in Canada. She lost. Unafraid, Serena pushed onward.

CHAMPION

In the next few years, Serena's powerful serves on the court led to success. In 1999, at age seventeen, she became the first African American woman to win a **Grand Slam** tournament in forty-one years. The following year, Serena and Venus played for the United States in the Olympics and won a gold medal as a doubles team.

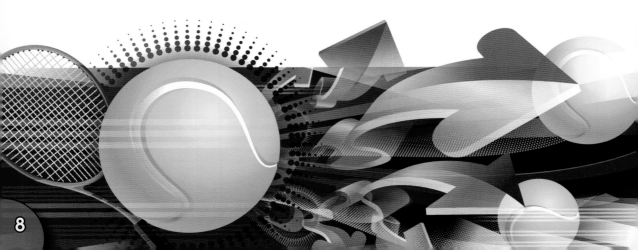

After Serena went pro, she didn't stop working hard. To become a master, she had to continue practicing every day!

Serena holds her trophy after winning the Italian Open in 2002.

Then, between 2002 and 2003, Serena won four Majors, or Grand Slam tournaments, in a row. These included the US Open, the French Open, Wimbledon, and the Australian Open. This became known as the

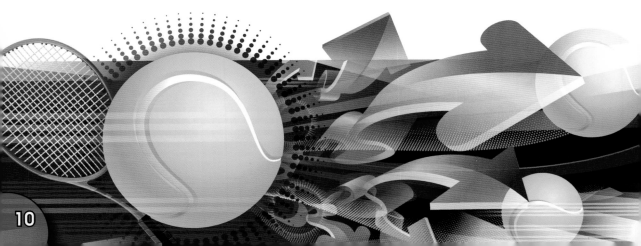

"Serena Slam"—and it would be a feat she'd complete again between 2014 and 2015.

HIGHS AND LOWS

But 2003 was also a difficult year for Serena. She had surgery on her left leg above her knee, and her grandmother died that summer. Worst of all, her oldest half sister, Yetunde Price, who was also her assistant, was killed in a shooting in Compton.

> Serena Says:
> "I practiced to play on the professional tour level, not the amateur, not the Tier 3 and 4 events. Once I make a decision, I never go back on it."

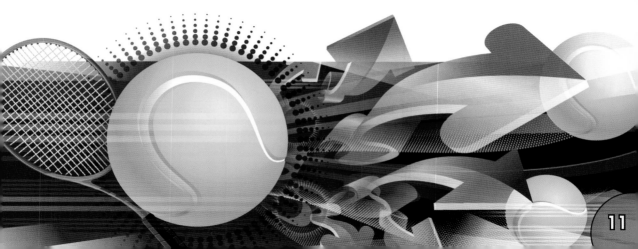

Serena doesn't spend all her time practicing. She attends charity events and celebrity parties and makes TV appearances.

Serena won Comeback Player of the Year when she returned to competing in 2004. But she spent 2005 and 2006 recovering from her losses on and off the court.

FUN FACT

After his daughters went pro, Richard Williams said, "Venus was going to be a great one and Serena was going to be the best one."

CHAPTER 3
POWER PAIR

While Serena succeeded as a tennis star, her sister did, too. At first, their father wouldn't enter them in the same tournaments so they wouldn't face one another. They'd grown up pushing each other in practice, but **competing** may have been hard on the sisters. Their first match was at the 1998 Australian Open, and Venus won. Since, Serena and her sister have competed at all of the Grand Slams and many other tournaments. Their matches are often for the top prize. They've even been ranked the top two in the world!

Serena and Venus face off against each other at the 2015 US Open.

SISTER SUCCESSES

Serena has spent much of her career working with her sister, too. In 2008, Serena and Venus won their second doubles gold medal against the Spanish team. They won again in 2012, becoming the first tennis pair to win Olympic doubles gold three times. Serena won the Olympic gold as a singles player in 2012, too. Serena said she was more excited about the doubles gold medal: "There's something about standing next to Venus and holding that gold medal."

Serena and Venus don't act like rivals except on the court. Some say tennis star Maria Sharapova is Serena's **rival** instead. In 2004, Sharapova upset Serena at the final of Wimbledon.

FUN FACT
Serena and Venus have met on the court almost thirty times, with Serena leading by just a few wins.

The Williams sisters pose with their Olympic gold medals in 2012.

However, while Maria Sharapova has been highly ranked during much of Serena's career, Serena has won almost all of their matches.

In 2016, Serena and Venus went to Rio de Janeiro, Brazil, to again represent the US on the Olympic tennis court. For the first time in the pair's Olympic history, they lost, 6–3, 6–4, to the

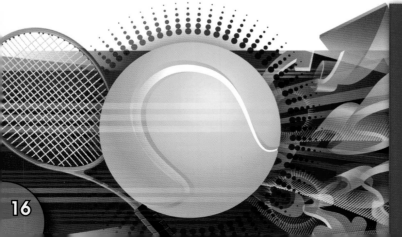

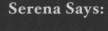

Serena Says:

"I don't know anyone out there who would get tired of playing with Venus Williams."

Czech team of Barbora Strycova and Lucie Safarova. But it's almost certain they'll be back in 2020, ready to win gold again.

In 2016, Serena won the Wimbledon singles tournament, as well as doubles with sister Venus.

CHAPTER 4
BEYOND TENNIS

Ruling the tennis court is just one way Serena has made her mark on the world. Serena has also come to be known for her fashion choices. After years of working with many clothing brands, Serena designed her own fashion line in 2014. She sometimes appears on the TV channel HSN to sell her creations. Serena has appeared on TV in several acting roles, too, including playing herself and doing voice acting for shows such as *The Legend of Korra.*

GIVING BACK

In addition, Serena has carried out years of charitable work through her organization, the Serena Williams Fund. The SW Fund works to help those affected by community violence and to make education

Serena Says:
"You can be strong, powerful, and beautiful at the same time. You can be amazing, and you can just be you."

available to everyone, no matter where they live. Serena teamed up with UNICEF in Africa in 2006 to help fight childhood diseases in Ghana.

More than a tennis pro, Serena loves fashion, too!

Serena is known for being glamorous off the court. Here, she poses at the *Vanity Fair* Oscar party in 2015.

She became a Goodwill Ambassador in 2011 and has supported UNICEF's work to offer schooling to children in Africa. These good works may last even longer than her records on the court.

LOOKING AHEAD

Serena's tennis career isn't over yet. She's already considered the best female tennis player ever, even after more than twenty years as a pro. She has said, though, "I know I can't play forever, but I feel like I want to and that's the hardest part."

It is important to Serena to help give children opportunities for better heath and education.

TIMELINE

1981 Serena Williams is born on September 26 in Saginaw, Michigan.

1995 Serena goes pro at age fourteen.

1999 Serena becomes the first African American woman to win a Grand Slam tournament in forty-one years.

2000 Serena and Venus win their first Olympic gold medals as a doubles team.

2008 Serena and Venus win their second Olympic gold medals.

2011 Serena becomes a UNICEF Goodwill Ambassador.

2012 The Williams sisters become the first pair to win three Olympic gold medals in doubles tennis. Serena also wins a singles gold medal.

2014 Serena first presents her clothing line at New York Fashion Week.

2016 Serena and Venus go to Rio de Janeiro to play in the 2016 Olympics.

LEARN MORE

BOOKS

Gagne, Tammy. *Day by Day with Serena Williams.* Hockessin, DE: Mitchell Lane Publishers, 2016.

Kortemeier, Todd. *Superstars of Pro Tennis.* Mankato, MN: Amicus High Interest, 2016.

Plowden, Martha Ward. *Famous Firsts of Women of Color.* Gretna, LA: Pelican Publishing Company, 2016.

WEBSITES

Serena Williams

serenawilliams.com

Keep up to date on news about Serena Williams on her website.

ESPN

espn.go.com/tennis/player/_/id/394/serena-williams

Find out the results of all Serena's matches and other tennis standings.

INDEX

Published in 2017 by Enslow Publishing, LLC.
101 W. 23rd Street, Suite 240, New York, NY 10011

Copyright © 2017 by Enslow Publishing, LLC.

Library of Congress Cataloging-in-Publication Data:
Names: Rajczak Nelson, Kristen, author.
Title: Serena Williams : tennis star / Kristen Rajczak Nelson.
Description: New York : Enslow Publishing, 2017. | Series: Junior biographies | Includes bibliographical references and index.
Identifiers: LCCN 2016020290| ISBN 9780766081826 (Library Bound) | ISBN 9780766081819 (Paperback) | ISBN 9780766082267 (6-pack)
Subjects: LCSH: Williams, Serena, 1981—Juvenile literature. | Tennis players—United States—Biography—Juvenile literature. | African American women tennis players—Biography—Juvenile literature.
Classification: LCC GV994.W55 R35 2017 | DDC 796.342092 [B] —dc23
LC record available at https://lccn.loc.gov/2016020290

Printed in China

To Our Readers: We have done our best to make sure all websites in this book were active and appropriate when we went to press. However, the author and the publisher have no control over and assume no liability for the material available on those websites or on any websites they may link to. Any comments or suggestions can be sent by e-mail to customerservice@enslow.com.

Photo Credits: Cover, p. 1 Matthew Lewis/Getty Images; p. 4 Harry How/Getty Images; p. 6 Ken Levine/Getty Images; p. 7 Ron Galella/Getty Images; p. 9 Simon Bruty/Sports Illustrated/Getty Images; p. 10 Alex Livesey/Getty Images; p. 12 Michael Caulfield Archive/WireImage/Getty Images; p. 14 Carlos M. Saavedra/Sports Illustrated/Getty Images; p. 16 Luis Acosta/AFP/Getty Images; p. 17 Karwai Tang/WireImage/Getty Images; p. 19 Thomas Concordia/WireImage/Getty Images; p. 20 Jon Kopaloff/FilmMagic/Getty Images; p. 21 Seyllou/AFP/Getty Images; back cover, interior pages (curves graphic) Alena Kazlouskaya/Shutterstock.com; interior pages (tennis graphic) derrrek/DigitalVision Vectors/Getty Images